verse books may be ordered through booksellers or by
contacting:

iUniverse
2021 Pine Lake Road, Suite 100
Lincoln, NE 68512
www.iuniverse.com
1-800-Authors (1-800-288-4677)

ause of the dynamic nature of the Internet, any Web addresses
or links contained in this book may have changed
since publication and may no longer be valid.

The views expressed in this work are solely those of the author
nd do not necessarily reflect the views of the publisher, and the
publisher hereby disclaims any responsibility for them.

ISBN: 978-0-595-47973-3 (pbk)
ISBN: 978-0-595-60070-0 (ebk)

Printed in the United States of America

Yellowstone National Park for Kids, Preteens, and Teenagers

Yell[

Natio.
for Kids,
and Tee

A Grande Guides
for Child.

Stephanie F. Del

iUniverse, Inc.
New York   Lincoln   Shanghai

To Mike, Sarah and Mark
(Old Faithful, Beehive, and Clepsydra Geysers)

Contents

NPS Photo

Preface

Yellowstone National Park for Kids, Preteens, and Teenagers is a guide, written especially for children and young adults, to help you make the most of your trip to America's first national park. It describes how Yellowstone was discovered and set aside as a national park. It explains the geology of Yellowstone so you will understand what causes the geysers, mudpots, and hot springs to bubble and erupt. It describes the types of wildlife you may see and it highlights some of the best hikes and natural wonders you can enjoy when you visit Yellowstone. Finally, at the end of the book, you can have some fun with a few word games and puzzles related to Yellowstone National Park. I wrote this book so my own children would have a fun filled, useful guide to Yellowstone and would learn to appreciate the park. I hope that you too will enjoy the book and learn enough about Yellowstone to develop a lifelong love of America's national parks.

Caution: All wildlife can be dangerous. Keep your distance and never approach or try to feed wild animals. Geyser basins are constantly changing. Boiling water lies just below the thin crust of most geyser basins. Many people have been severely burned when they have fallen through the fragile surface. Some people have even died from falling into hydrothermal features. For your own safety, obey all signs at Yellowstone and stay on the trails and boardwalks.

> *Did you know that Yellowstone National Park is about the same size as the entire state of Connecticut?*

Introduction to Yellowstone National Park

Yellowstone National Park is a great place for children, regardless of your interests and hobbies. If you enjoy science, you can study the geology of the park. If you enjoy history, there is so much to learn about Yellowstone and about the United States. If you like art or photography, bring your sketch book or camera and find a quiet place to draw or take pictures. If you dream of becoming an author, try writing some poems or short stories about your experiences in Yellowstone.

Yellowstone is a unique and special place. It is filled with wildlife (including bears, elk, moose, wolves, and more), bubbling mudpots, and geysers that rumble and erupt, spitting water high into the air like powerful fountains. Yellowstone is located in the northwest part of the United States. Most of the park is in the state of Wyoming with small parts of it overflowing into Idaho and Montana.

Yellowstone is America's first national park, founded over one hundred years ago. During the past hundred years, buildings have been built, roads have been paved, and boardwalks and trails have been constructed. But despite these changes, Yellowstone today is still very much like it was a hundred years ago. Most of the geysers and hot springs are as beautiful and powerful now as they were when the park was first founded and the wildlife in the park continues to flourish. This is due to the efforts of people who are dedicated to the preservation of Yellowstone. It's up to all of us to preserve and protect Yellowstone and all our national parks. You can help by staying on the trails and boardwalks, putting garbage (including gum and food) into trash cans, and by keeping a safe distance from all wildlife. If we all do our part, Yellowstone will be as beautiful in the future as it is today.

Shake, Rattle, and Roll:
The Geology of Yellowstone

Yellowstone National Park is one of the biggest active volcanoes in the entire world. Some people use the term "super volcano" to describe Yellowstone. But relax, it's not your typical volcano on the verge of erupting. Yellowstone doesn't look or act like a typical volcano. Most volcanoes appear as a single mountain. Yellowstone is actually a caldera (pronounced kal-der-uh), which is a depression or large shallow hole in the surface of the earth. The Yellowstone caldera covers fifteen hundred square miles so it is much, much larger than a typical volcano. When you visit Yellowstone, you actually go *inside* the volcanic caldera to view the geysers and other attractions! In some areas, the magma chamber, or large underground pool of hot molten rock, is only a few miles below the surface of the ground you are standing on. Sound scary? Not really.

The last major volcanic eruption at Yellowstone was 640,000 years ago. Scientists say that before another eruption, we would have warning signs. Geologists who study Yellowstone use satellites and other technology to monitor volcanic activity and look for changes in underground hot spots. Hot spots are fixed places under the surface of the earth where rocks melt to make magma. Changes in these hot spots would show that molten rock was being pushed toward the surface of the earth warning us that an eruption would occur soon. The geologic activity at Yellowstone has not changed significantly over the past thirty years since scientists first started monitoring it. So relax and enjoy the beauty of Yellowstone.

Yellowstone has about ten thousand hot springs and geysers. These geothermal features are proof that there is active volcanic magma below the surface. The word geothermal means related to the heat inside the earth ("geo" means related to the earth and "thermal" means heat). The volcanic magma within the earth' provides fuel for the geysers, mudpots, and hot springs by heating the water inside them to extremely high temperatures. Yellowstone has four types of geothermal features: hot springs, geysers, mudpots, and fumaroles.

Hot springs: When it rains or snows, the water slips through layers of rock as it sinks deep into the ground. Eventually that water becomes heated by rocks that have been heated by the magma under the surface of the earth. The hot water boils and rises back up toward the surface. Some of Yellowstone's hot springs are quiet, calm pools while others produce flowing water. You can see Yellowstone's largest hot spring, Grand Prismatic Spring, in the Midway Geyser Basin. This hot spring is 370 feet in diameter and more than 121 feet deep.

Right: Riverside Geyser in the Upper Geyer Basin erupts into the Firehole River. NPS Photo by Jim Peaco.

Below: Grand Prismatic Spring in the Midway Geyser Basin is the largest hot spring in Yellowstone. NPS Photo by Al Mebane.

Geysers: Geysers are similar to hot springs. The difference is that as the heated water rises back toward the surface, it collects in gaps called rock pockets and it can't move freely, causing pressure to build. The temperature of the water gets higher and higher until eventually it boils. Steam rises quickly, taking the water from the rock pockets with it. When the pressure is released, the water explodes out through the opening in the ground and continues until the steamy groundwater is gone. Some eruptions last only a few minutes while others can last an hour or more. When the eruption is over, the rock pocket refills with groundwater and the cycle begins again.

There are two types of geysers. Fountain type geysers shoot water up from a pool, often spraying it in different directions. Cone type geysers erupt in a straight, nozzle-like formation, like water coming out of a hose. The cone on this type of geyser helps to streamline the water so it doesn't spread in many directions as it erupts.

There are many geysers in Yellowstone but only a few geysers are predicted regularly by the park staff. Examples of geysers that can be predicted are Castle Geyser, Grand Geyser, Daisy Geyser, Riverside Geyser, and Old Faithful. The world's tallest geyser is Steamboat Geyser in the Norris Geyser Basin but it is very unpredictable. It once went fifty years without erupting but when it does erupt, it can shoot to heights of 300–400 feet!

Think of Yellowstone's geysers as each having its own personality. Some are reliable and consistent like a good friend. Some are loud and have lots of energy like a silly

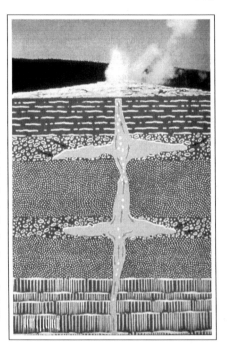

Right: Rain water and melted snow seep into the ground. The water is warmed by the hot magma. In a geyser, narrow passages and gaps in the rocks create pressure. When the pressure is finally released, the water explodes through the opening in the ground, spurting water high into the air like a fountain. NPS diagram.

little sister or brother. Others are calm and quiet and make you feel relaxed like your favorite relative. As you learn about Yellowstone's geysers and watch them erupt, see who they remind you of. Which one do you think is most like you?

Mudpots: Mudpots are similar to hot springs except that the groundwater has dissolved rocks into clay, creating mud. High levels of acid in the water help to dissolve the rocks quickly. The color of the mud often varies depending on the minerals that are in the rocks. You can see two large mudpots in the Artist Paint Pot section of the park near Madison.

Fumaroles: Fumaroles (pronounced fyoo-muh-rohls) are vents in the earth's crust. Fumaroles are also called steam vents. With fumaroles there is less water than with geysers or hot springs. Since the supply of water is lower, it is all turned into steam when it comes in contact with the hot rocks that have been heated by the magma. The steam escapes through the vents or cracks in the earth's crust. Sometimes it escapes with such force that it creates a loud hissing sound. Roaring Mountain in the Norris Geyser Basin contains many fumaroles.

While Yellowstone's geothermal features are beautiful to see, they can also be very dangerous. The water in the hot springs and geysers is hot enough to burn or scald you. It is important to stay on the trails and boardwalks and obey all signs. The ground or crust around the geysers and hot springs is often thin and could crack and collapse if you get too close. You should also protect your camera and binoculars when you are close to a geyser or hot spring. The steam and spray from the hot water can damage the lens so keep these items covered or in a case when you are not using them.

The geothermal features in Yellowstone are home to microscopic living organisms called thermophiles. The **word thermophile means heat lover** ("thermo" means heat and "phile" means lover). Microscopic means these organisms can only be seen with a microscope because they are too small to be seen with just your eyes. There are thermophiles in many of the geysers and hot springs in Yellowstone. Different types of thermophiles create different colors in the water. Some are yellow, orange, or red and others appear blue or green. Some of the organisms that live in Yellowstone's rivers can cause serious illnesses or diseases, so you should never drink from or swim in Yellowstone's rivers.

When visiting Yellowstone, you may notice a bad smell that is often described as a rotten egg smell. The smell is from small amounts of hydrogen sulfide gas or sulfur that rises through the cracks in the ground. It's not dangerous but can smell pretty strong and gross sometimes. Try plugging your nose and breathing through your mouth!

Believe It or Not:
A Lesson in Yellowstone's History

Native Americans were the first people to live in the Yellowstone area. In fact, the Native Americans are credited with naming the Yellowstone River "Mi tse a da zi," which means rock yellow river. Later, fur trappers translated this to yellow rock or yellow stone. Many people believe that the river was named for the yellow rocks seen in the Grand Canyon of the Yellowstone but no one knows for sure.

In the early 1800s, President Thomas Jefferson asked Meriwether Lewis and William Clark to lead an expedition across the west. One of the men in the Discovery Corps led by Lewis and Clark was John Colter. The Lewis and Clark expedition did not pass through Yellowstone but John Colter later explored the area while hunting for furs in 1807.

Imagine yourself as John Colter in the early 1800s. There were no cars, buildings, boardwalks, signs, or other visitors in Yellowstone. Imagine stumbling upon an erupting geyser or hissing fumarole. Never having seen or heard of these geothermal features, Colter must have been surprised and even frightened by his discovery. When you go to Yellowstone, find a quiet, peaceful place and try to imagine what it must have been like to be John Colter in 1807.

After traveling hundreds of miles through Yellowstone, Colter returned to civilization to describe what he had seen. People did not believe his reports of geysers, steaming pools of water, and bubbling pots of mud. Most people thought he was crazy. Over the next forty years, many other trappers and mountain men made similar reports of boiling mud, geysers, and steaming rivers, but most people did not believe these reports either. It wasn't until the 1860s, more than fifty years later, that people began to believe the stories about Yellowstone and have an interest in exploring the area.

In 1871, Dr. Ferdinand V. Hayden gathered a team including geologists, zoologists, botanists, a photographer named William H. Jackson, and an artist named Thomas Moran. This team explored the Yellowstone area and brought back pictures, drawings and stories that helped prove that the natural wonders of Yellowstone existed. Hayden prepared a report and urged Congress to set aside the Yellowstone region as America's first national park. In March 1872, President Ulysses S. Grant signed an act into law creating Yellowstone National Park. By setting aside this

Sketches and paintings from the late 1800s by artist, Thomas Moran helped convince Congress and President Grant to designate Yellowstone as a National Park. Above: NPS sketch of Castle Geyser by Thomas Moran. Right: NPS sketch of the Lower Falls of the Yellowstone River by Thomas Moran.

land as a national park, it has been preserved for over one hundred years, still appearing today much as it did when John Colter first explored the land in the early 1800s.

Something that has changed the appearance of the park over the past hundred years is fire. During the summer of 1988, eight large forest fires swept through Yellowstone burning more than one third of the park. The fires burned almost all summer while 25,000 firefighters helped fight the blazes. It was the biggest and most expensive fire in history. At times the fire jumped across rivers as winds blew hot, burning embers throughout the park.

When the fires finally burned out, people worried that the park had been destroyed and that many animals had died. In fact, only 261 large mammals had died. Most of them died from the smoke while others were killed by fire trucks in road accidents. While it is sad that some animals died in the fire, the overall number was very small compared to the total number of animals in Yellowstone. Also, even though many trees burned, they did not go to waste. The ashes of these trees helped to nourish the soil and as a result of the fires, Yellowstone became a more open, sunnier place. The fires also helped certain trees to produce seedlings. Lodgepole pines have cones that are glued shut by resin. They need the heat of a wildfire to melt down the resin, allowing the cone to pop open so the seeds within can be spread. So in a sense the fires of 1988 didn't destroy Yellowstone National Park, they just changed it.

> *Did you know that bison can run up to thirty miles per hour? That's a lot faster than you or I can run!*

Bison and Elk and Bears ... Oh My!
Yellowstone's Wildlife

Yellowstone offers some of the best opportunities to see wildlife in the United States. Bring your binoculars and you may see wolves, grizzly bears, bison, elk, coyotes, bighorn sheep, and more. It is important to keep in mind that the animals in Yellowstone are wild and can be dangerous. Keep a safe distance from all wild animals and make noise when you are hiking. Even small and gentle looking animals like squirrels and deer can carry diseases and be dangerous. Also, remember that feeding animals and birds in Yellowstone is against the law. This chapter describes some of the animals you may encounter in Yellowstone. You can keep track of the wildlife you see with the checklist at the end of this book.

Bison: In the early 1800s there were about sixty-five million bison in North America. However, because of hunting and poaching, by the early 1900s there were fewer than a thousand with only about twenty-five in

Yellowstone. Efforts were made to protect the bison and by 1954 there were about fifteen hundred in Yellowstone. Since that time, the bison in the park have continued to flourish and there are now many bison in Yellowstone. It is a good reminder that animals often need to be protected to avoid becoming an endangered or extinct species.

An adult bison can be over six feet tall and weigh over two thousand pounds. Baby bison, or calves, are born in April and May. If you visit the park during late May or early June, you will most likely see many baby bison. Bison can be seen in many different parts of the park including the Lamar Valley, Hayden Valley, and along the Madison, Firehole, and Gibbon Rivers.

Grizzly Bears and Black Bears: Both grizzly bears and black bears can weigh 500–600 pounds and can run up to thirty miles per hour for short stretches. They are omnivorous, which means they eat both plants and other animals (small rodents, elk, and bison carcasses). Grizzly bears are typically larger than black bears and usually have a large shoulder hump. Both grizzly bears and black bears can be seen in many sections of the park. The Hayden Valley, Lamar Valley, and the area around the Fishing Bridge are usually good spots to see a bear. If you really want to see one, stop by one of the Visitor Centers and ask a park ranger if there have been any recent sightings. He or she may be able to give you advice to aid in your search.

Above: A mother bison and her calf in the Lamar Valley in Yellowstone National Park. NPS photo by Jim Peaco. Below: A pronghorn antelope, the fastest land animal in North America. NPS photo by William W. Dunmire.

Pronghorn: Pronghorn antelope are the fastest land animals in North America. They can run up to sixty miles per hour. Pronghorn typically travel in small groups for safety. Sometimes they can be found in the hills behind the Mammoth Hot Springs and in the Lamar Valley.

Elk: Elk can typically be seen throughout Yellowstone year round. During the late spring and summer, elk can often be seen traveling in large herds. Elk retain their antlers through the winter and shed them in the spring to grow new antlers. They resemble deer but are much bigger. The area around the Mammoth Hot Springs is a great place to see elk from a relatively close range. As with any wildlife in the park, they can become agitated by people so keep your distance.

Moose: While moose are not as common in Yellowstone as bison or elk, visitors often can see them in the park. Moose are members of the deer family but can weigh up to one thousand pounds. Moose feed on aquatic plants (plants that grow in the water) and can often be seen in marshy areas or in lakes and streams. If you visit nearby Grand Teton National Park, the lakes and rivers there are good places to spot a moose.

Coyotes: Most coyotes only weigh about thirty-five pounds and are smaller than wolves. Their fur is typically grey, sometimes with a reddish tint. Coyotes have a bushy tail and often roam alone. Coyotes usually eat small rodents like squirrels and rabbits. Coyotes can be seen roaming in almost any part of Yellowstone, especially at dusk. They can often be seen from the road, from the comfort of your family car.

Above: An elk searches for food in the winter in Yellowstone. NPS photo by George Marler. Below: Two male elk with their antlers locked, proving their strength. NPS photo by J. Schmidt.

Wolves: Wolves often weigh twice what coyotes weigh and stand taller. They can be tan, white, grey or silver, and even black. Unlike coyotes, wolves typically travel, hunt, and live in packs. The pack is a social unit that is like an extended family.

The history of wolves in Yellowstone is an unusual one. Wolves lived in Yellowstone when the park was established in 1872. In an effort to control the wolves, between 1914 and 1926 more than one hundred wolves were killed in the park. By the 1940s, wolf packs were rarely reported and by the 1970s, there were no wolves left in Yellowstone. The National Park Service realized it needed to reintroduce the wolves to Yellowstone. Experts agreed that bringing wolves back into Yellowstone would help control the growth of other animal species and would return Yellowstone to a more natural, balanced state. So in 1995, fourteen wolves from separate packs were captured in Canada and transported to Yellowstone. Since this time, the wolves have thrived and can once again be seen in the park. For the best chance of seeing the wolves, visit the Lamar Valley area early in the morning or at dusk.

Bighorn sheep: Bighorn sheep have small, muscular bodies. The most distinct characteristic is the male bighorn sheep's large curved horns that curl back over his ears. Female bighorn sheep have smaller horns. Male bighorn sheep are known for having head-to-head combat. Bighorn sheep are very agile and can balance on small rocky ledges. As a result, they are often hard to see since they are not typically out in open meadows where they can be seen easily from the road.

Above: A wolf rests in the snow in Yellowstone. Wolves can sometimes be seen in the Lamar Valley area. NPS photo by Doug Smith. Below: Bighorn sheep causing a traffic jam on a busy road in the park. NPS photo by Jim Peaco.

Eagles: Both bald eagles and golden eagles can be seen in Yellowstone. They eat fish, waterfowl, rodents, and small mammals. A golden eagle can be identified by its dark feathers with bright gold on the back of its head. A golden eagle has a smaller head, bill, and neck than a bald eagle. The tail of a golden eagle is longer than the tail of a bald eagle. An adult bald eagle is easily identified by its pure, white head and brownish black body. The bald eagle was once listed as an endangered species but the population has since increased significantly. Eagles can be seen along the banks of the rivers in Yellowstone or soaring above mountain meadows. The areas around the Madison River and Lake Yellowstone are particularly good places to watch for eagles.

Osprey: Osprey are medium sized birds of prey that eat fish. They are also sometimes called fish hawks. They are brown on the upper parts of their bodies and wings and mostly white on the head and under parts, with a brown eye patch. They can sometimes be seen diving for fish in the rivers or lakes of Yellowstone or perched on top of their large nests on trees and tall poles in and around the park.

Trumpeter Swans: Trumpeter swans are large waterfowl, often growing even larger than bald eagles. Their wingspan can be seven feet across and they can weigh up to thirty pounds. The trumpeter swan gets its name from its trumpet-like call. North America is the only continent where trumpeter swans live naturally. In the mid 1800s, trumpeter swans were nearly extinct. They were often killed for their large feathers to be used in women's hats. Fewer than one hundred birds remained when Congress established a wildlife preserve to help the swans recover from near extinction. Trumpeter swans can sometimes be seen on the Madison and Firehole Rivers.

> *Did you know that Yellowstone National Park contains more than 10,000 geothermal features?*

Are We There Yet?
Things to Do and See in Yellowstone

So are you ready to start touring Yellowstone? Great! This chapter is divided into ten sections, one for each of the major sections of the park. Each section includes a description of some of the most popular things to see and do. In addition, each section has a "Highlights" box that lists the most popular attractions. You can use this tool to quickly locate things that interest you and to keep track of what you've seen during your trip.

There are five entrances into Yellowstone. Each entrance offers something different to experience. It is a good idea to stop at one of the Visitor Centers on your way into the park. There are nine Visitor Centers throughout Yellowstone. The Visitor Centers offer short movies, free and inexpensive maps, hiking guides, wildlife tips, and other materials. Many of the Visitor Centers also have interesting exhibits about Yellowstone's geology, history, wildlife, and the fires of 1988. In addition, the Park Rangers can provide valuable information to make your visit more fun.

At the Visitor Centers, kids between age five and twelve can buy a Junior Ranger newspaper for about three dollars. After completing specific activities in the newspaper, you will become a Junior Ranger and you will receive a special patch. You can also buy a National Park Passport, which you can stamp yourself at any of the Visitor Centers. Almost all national parks in the United States offer the cancellation stamps for free. These stamps are a great reminder of your national park visits. Hint: It's a good idea to check the cancellation stamp to make sure the date is correct before stamping it in your book!

The heart of Yellowstone is a large, looping road that forms a figure eight. It is called the Grand Loop Road. As you travel along the Grand Loop Road there are many things to see and do. This chapter describes some of the most popular sights in Yellowstone National Park, especially for kids, preteens, and teenagers.

The Upper Geyser Basin and Old Faithful: The Upper Geyser Basin contains over 150 thermal features within only one square mile. This means you can see a variety of geysers and hot springs without walking very far. The Upper Geyser Basin has

Highlights
❏ Old Faithful Geyser
❏ Morning Glory Pool
❏ Riverside Geyser
❏ Old Faithful Inn

boardwalks and paved trails that will lead you from one geyser or hot spring to the next.

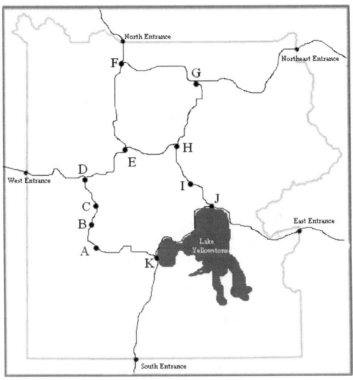

A—The Upper Geyser Basin and Old Faithful
B—The Midway Geyser Basin
C—The Lower Geyser Basin
D—Madison
E—Norris
F—Mammoth Hot Springs
G—Tower-Roosevelt
H—The Canyon Area
I—Hayden Valley and the Mud Volcano
J—The Fishing Bridge
K—The West Thumb Geyser Basin

The Upper Geyser Basin is home to Old Faithful, Yellowstone's most well known geyser. It was named in 1870 for its consistent and predictable performance. Old Faithful erupts more frequently than any of the other big geysers, but it is not the largest or most regular geyser in Yellowstone. On average, Old Faithful erupts about every ninety minutes. Most eruptions last just a few minutes and reach heights of over one hundred feet. Old Faithful is still as spectacular and predictable as it was a hundred years ago. For a different view of Old Faithful, try hiking up the Observation Point Loop Trail. On this trail you can climb the hill behind Old Faithful to Observation Point. From here you will be 250 feet above Old Faithful and will have a great view of the entire Upper Geyser Basin.

The Upper Geyser Basin is home to many other geysers as well. Giantess Geyser only erupts a few times each year but when it does, the ground shakes from underground steam explosions. Castle Geyser has a large cone and may be the oldest geyser in the basin. Grand Geyser is the tallest predictable geyser in the world and it erupts every seven to fifteen hours with powerful bursts. Daisy Geyser is unique because it erupts on an angle, rather than straight up into the air. It is predictable with eruptions occurring every 90–115 minutes. Beehive Geyser typically erupts twice each day and lasts only about four or five minutes. During an eruption, the narrow cone acts like a nozzle, focusing the water column to heights of about 150 feet. Stop in the Visitor Center in the Old Faithful area and the Park Rangers can tell you if Beehive

Right: A magnificent eruption of Old Faithful in the Upper Geyser Basin. NPS photo by Jim Peaco.

Below: Visitors gaze into the clear waters of Morning Glory Pool. NPS photo by Ed Austin, Herb Jones.

Geyser or Grand Geyser is likely to erupt soon. If so, they are both worth seeing and are treats that not all visitors to Yellowstone get to see.

Along the bank of the Firehole River in the Upper Geyser Basin, you can find Riverside Geyser. It erupts every five or six hours for about twenty minutes each time. During its eruptions, a column of water shoots out over the river making this one of the best geysers to photograph. An interesting fact about Riverside Geyser is that it has an "indicator." An indicator is a hint or clue that the geyser is about to erupt. With Riverside Geyser, the indicator is a runoff of water over the edge of the geyser's cone for an hour or two before each eruption. Many geysers have similar indicators that they are about to erupt.

Morning Glory Pool was named in the 1880s because it looked like a colorful morning glory flower. However, this pool is no longer as beautiful as it was a hundred years ago. Unfortunately, people threw coins, trash, rocks, and logs into the pool, which became stuck in the sides and vents of the spring. This caused the pool's temperature to decrease slightly. Over time, as the temperature dropped, Morning Glory's appearance changed. It is a good reminder of how fragile nature can be. We all need to respect the attractions at Yellowstone and other parks so children of the future will be able to enjoy these natural wonders.

In addition to the natural wonders near Old Faithful, you may also enjoy seeing some of the man-made attractions in the area. The Old Faithful Inn is definitely something worth seeing. In fact, it is a historic landmark. It was built over one hundred years ago. One of the most impressive features is the lobby, which is seven stories high! It has several balconies and even a "crow's nest," a small landing near the roof where musicians played during the early days of the inn. The lobby also has a huge stone fireplace with a beautiful old wrought iron clock above it. You can even go outside to the porch where you can relax and watch Old Faithful erupt. On a cool evening, the porch is a great spot to sit and enjoy a cup of hot chocolate.

The Midway Geyser Basin: The Midway Geyser Basin contains a small collection of thermal features. Despite its small size, the Midway Geyser Basin contains two of

> **Highlights**
> ❑ Grand Prismatic Spring
> ❑ Excelsior Geyser

the largest hot springs in the world—Grand Prismatic Spring and Excelsior Geyser. Grand Prismatic Spring is nearly 370 feet in diameter. It is the largest hot spring in Yellowstone and one of the largest in the entire world. Grand Prismatic Spring is named for its beautiful colors, caused by thermophiles living in the hot water. The center is deep blue followed by pale blue toward the edge. Along the border, green alga fades into yellow and orange then red marks the outer border. Steam often makes it difficult to appreciate the bright colors. Excelsior Geyser was once the largest geyser in the world. However, it no longer erupts to amazing heights but rather, constantly spills boiling water into the Firehole River.

The Lower Geyser Basin and Firehole Lake Drive: A few miles north of the Upper Geyser Basin is the Lower Geyser Basin. The Fountain Paint Pot Trail is one of the main attractions in the Lower Geyser Basin. Here you can see bubbling mudpots, hot springs, and more geysers. In the spring and early summer, the mudpots are thin and watery from rain and snow. By late summer, the mud is often thick and can splatter over the rails along the side of the trail. In the geyser area of the Fountain Paint Pot Trail there are six smaller geysers. You can view all six from a scenic overlook along the trail. Twig Geyser's eruptions last over an hour. Morning Geyser rarely erupts but when it does, water can spray up and out over a hundred feet in every direction. Clepsydra Geyser performs almost nonstop, splashing water out of several vents as it erupts.

> ### Highlights
> ❑ Fountain Paint Pot Trail
> ❑ Great Fountain Geyser
> ❑ Firehole Lake Drive

Also in this section of the park is a one way road named Firehole Lake Drive. Along this road, there are several geysers worth seeing. Great Fountain Geyser erupts every eight to twelve hours, spraying water over one hundred feet in the air. The White Dome Geyser and Pink Cone Geyser can also be seen from this one way, loop road. White Dome Geyser has probably been erupting for hundreds of years, based on the size of its large cone. It erupts about every thirty minutes to heights of about thirty feet. You can watch

Pink Cone Geyser from your car. In fact, when they built the road in the 1930s, they built it right across part of this geyser's mound. But it hasn't affected the performance of Pink Cone Geyser. It erupts about every six to twenty hours.

Madison Area and the Artist Paint Pot Trail: The Firehole Canyon Drive near Madison twists along the banks of the Firehole River, one of the cleanest and most pristine rivers in the park. This drive takes you past ancient lava flows and near Firehole Falls.

Highlights

❑ Artist Paint Pot Trail

❑ Harlequin Lake Trail

❑ Two Ribbons Trail

❑ Gibbon Falls

Firehole Falls is a scenic waterfall, about forty feet high.

The Artist Paint Pot Trail near Madison is a one-mile walk that is good for children of all ages. At the end of the trail you will find some of the most colorful hot springs as well as a few mudpots at the top of the hill. The trail allows you to get close to the mudpots so watch out for flying mud! This is also a good place to view the damage from the fires of 1988.

Two other nice hikes in this area are the Harlequin Lake Trail and the Two Ribbons Trail. The Harlequin Lake Trail is an easy one-mile hike through a forest of burned lodgepole pines. You won't see harlequin ducks here but may see other waterfowl. Since this trail brings you to a marshy lake, you may also find mosquitoes so bring your bug repellant. The Two Ribbons Trail travels about one mile along boardwalks. On this trail you can see examples of how the forest recovers after a fire.

Also in the Madison area, you will find Gibbon Falls. Gibbon Falls is at edge of the Yellowstone caldera. If you look across the road from the falls, the rock wall you see is actually the inner rim of the volcanic caldera. You can enjoy the falls from the road or take a short walk to the observation point for a better view.

Norris Area and the Museum of the National Park Ranger: The Norris Geyser Basin is the hottest and oldest of the thermal areas in Yellowstone. It is also one of the most active earthquake zones in the park. Dirt and boardwalk trails encircle the parts of the basin that are safe for visitors. In this area, you can see Steamboat Geyser (the world's tallest geyser when it erupts) as well as many other geysers, fumaroles, and hot springs.

Highlights
❑ Steamboat Geyser
❑ Ice Lake Trail
❑ Roaring Mountain
❑ Museum of the National Park Ranger

Another nice trail in this section of the park is the Ice Lake Trail. The Ice Lake Trail is an easy one-mile round-trip hike that travels through a forest of lodgepole pines toward Ice Lake. Roaring Mountain, just north of the Norris Geyser Basin on the Grand Loop Road, is another interesting stop. It contains many fumaroles and steam vents. Roaring Mountain was named for the loud hissing sounds that could be heard more than a mile away. However, it no longer roars and is actually rather quiet now.

The Museum of the National Park Ranger is near the entrance to Norris Campground. The museum is in a beautiful, old log building that was built in 1908 as a station for soldiers on patrol. The displays in the museum tell the history of the National Park Service, focusing on the men and women who have helped to protect our national parks throughout history. The museum is staffed by retired National Park Service employees who often have interesting stories about Yellowstone.

Mammoth Hot Springs Area and the Roosevelt Arch: The Mammoth Hot Springs Area is in the Northwest corner of Yellowstone National Park. The hot springs here are different from any other thermal features you will see in Yellowstone. Under the ground are thick layers of sedimentary limestone that

Highlights
❑ Liberty Cap
❑ Minerva Spring
❑ Fort Yellowstone
❑ Roosevelt Arch

were deposited there millions of years ago. As ground water from rain and melting snow seeps into the ground, carbon dioxide dissolves in the hot water. This hot, acidic liquid dissolves the limestone as it comes back up to the surface. When it is exposed to the air, the limestone again becomes a solid mineral that gets deposited as something called travertine. The travertine is what forms the terraces or layers that build up. Fresh travertine is white in color and becomes gray as it weathers.

The Liberty Cap and Minerva Spring and Terrace are two highlights in this section of the park. The Liberty Cap was named because it resembles the caps worn by colonial soldiers in the Revolutionary War. It is a tall cone that was formed by hot water that repeatedly deposited thick layers of travertine in one place. It continued to grow for many years but is now inactive. The Minerva Spring is one of the most beautiful and colorful terraces in the Mammoth area. When it is active, the travertine can build up as much as six to eight inches per year! As the water cools, an alga grows creating colors of red, orange, green, and yellow in the terrace runoffs.

The Mammoth Hot Springs area is important from a historical standpoint since the Fort Yellowstone buildings are located here. These were some of the first buildings to be built in Yellowstone. The Fort Yellowstone buildings originally housed army soldiers who were stationed in Yellowstone to help protect the park from vandals and poachers. The army was present in the park for thirty years. The Albright Visitor Center, which includes a museum, is one of the original Fort Yellowstone buildings.

The Roosevelt Arch is located at the north entrance to Yellowstone National Park, just a few miles beyond the Mammoth Hot Springs. The arch, which is made of rock, is fifty feet high and the main opening is large enough for cars and motor homes to drive through. The top of the arch is carved with the words *For the benefit and enjoyment of the people.* The cornerstone of the arch was laid

Right: The Liberty Cap in the Mammoth Hot Springs area was named because it resembles the caps worn by colonial soldiers in the Revolutionary War. NPS photo by Harlan Kredit.

Below: Travertine on the terraces of the Minerva Spring can build up as much as six to eight inches per year. NPS photo by J. Schmidt.

by President Theodore Roosevelt while he was in the park on vacation.

The Tower-Roosevelt Area and Lamar Valley: The Tower-Roosevelt section of the park and the Lamar Valley are in the Northeast corner of Yellowstone. Here you can find more waterfalls, wildlife, and petrified trees.

> Highlights
> ❏ The Petrified Tree
> ❏ Tower Falls
> ❏ Wildlife

Petrified trees are trees that have been turned into rock because all organic material has been replaced by minerals. The petrified trees in Yellowstone were created when they were slowly buried by volcanic ash. One petrified tree is located near the Lost Lake trailhead, close to the main road between Mammoth Hot Springs and Tower-Roosevelt. It is behind a fence to protect it. There used to be two other petrified trees here, but they were removed, piece by piece, by careless park visitors who took pieces home as souvenirs. There are other petrified trees on Specimen Ridge but they are harder to find. In fact, Specimen Ridge is the largest group of petrified trees in the world.

Tower Falls is a beautiful waterfall that is 132 feet high. You can see the falls from above from the parking area or can walk down a steep half-mile trail to the base, or bottom of the falls. On a hot day, the mist from the falls may cool you off at the bottom.

Above: The Fort Yellowstone buildings originally housed soldiers who were stationed in Yellowstone to help protect the park. NPS photo by RC Townsend. Below: The Roosevelt Arch is located at the north entrance to the park. NPS photo by RG Johnsson.

During the summer you can enjoy a western cookout in the Tower-Roosevelt area. You can either ride a horse or take a covered wagon to Pleasant Valley where the cookout is held. The cookout includes authentic western food (steak, corn bread, and baked beans) and some type of entertainment (usually a cowboy singer).

The Lamar Valley is located just east of Tower-Roosevelt. Here you will often see elk, bison, osprey, bald eagles, pronghorn antelope, moose, and bears. The best time to see wildlife in the Lamar Valley is in the early morning or late evening. This is also a great place to look for wolves so bring your binoculars!

The Canyon Area: The Grand Canyon of the Yellowstone is the main attraction in the Canyon Area of the park. The canyon is about twenty miles long and was formed by erosion caused by the rushing waters of the Yellowstone River.

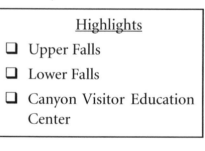

Highlights
- ❑ Upper Falls
- ❑ Lower Falls
- ❑ Canyon Visitor Education Center

There are two major waterfalls in the canyon. The Upper Falls is 109 feet high and can be seen from the Brink of the Upper Falls Trail and from Uncle Tom's Trail. The Lower Falls is 308 feet high and can be seen from Lookout Point, Red Rock Point, Artist Point, Brink of the Lower Falls Trail, and from various points on the South Rim Trail. The Lower Falls is twice as high as Niagara Falls.

Be sure to visit the Canyon Visitor Education Center where you can learn more about the geology of Yellowstone. This unique exhibit has a room-size model of Yellowstone that shows the park's volcanic eruptions, lava flows, glaciers, and earthquake faults. There is also a huge rotating globe highlighting volcanic hotspots and one of the world's largest lava lamps that shows how magma rises.

Hayden Valley and the Fishing Bridge Area: Hayden Valley is one of the best places in Yellowstone to view wildlife. It is an excellent place to look for bears, bald eagles, and other birds of prey. Coyotes can almost always be seen in the Hayden Valley. Hayden Valley is also where you will find the Mud Volcano and Sulfur Caldron. Short trails bring you past mudpots and strange looking and sounding fumaroles that are worth a quick stop. Walk past the Dragon's Mouth and you may hear it gurgling and belching at you!

> ### Highlights
> ❑ Fishing Bridge
> ❑ Pelican Creek Trail
> ❑ Mud Volcano and Sulfur Caldron
> ❑ Wildlife

Just south of Hayden Valley is the Fishing Bridge. Yellowstone's original Fishing Bridge was built in 1902 and was then rebuilt in 1937. For years it was a very popular place to fish but it was closed to fishing in 1973. Now it is a great place to watch for fish. Often you can see large groups of cutthroat trout in the clear waters. Cutthroat trout were given their name for the slashes of red below their mouths. The surrounding forests and meadows are prime grizzly bear territory too so keep your eyes open!

An easy hike in this area is the Pelican Creek Trail. This trail passes through a forest to the shore of a lake then loops back along the Pelican Creek. Watch for different birds in the marshy areas near the creek.

Yellowstone Lake and the West Thumb Geyser Basin:

Highlights
❑ Yellowstone Lake
❑ Fishing Cone
❑ Duck Lake Trail

Yellowstone Lake is the park's largest lake. It is twenty miles long and fourteen miles wide with one hundred miles of shoreline. Yellowstone Lake remains cold year round and even freezes over completely in the winter. Despite an average temperature of only forty-one degrees, the lake has the largest population of wild cutthroat trout in North America.

The deepest part of Yellowstone Lake is called the West Thumb (because the lake is shaped like a hand with this part as the thumb). Along this section of the lake is a small geyser basin with boardwalks that run right along the shore of the lake. There are several interesting and colorful hot springs, fumaroles, geysers, and mudpots along this trail. One of the most famous attractions is the Fishing Cone. Early visitors to the park claimed that you could use your fishing pole to catch a fish in the lake then quickly dip it into the boiling waters of the Fishing Cone

Right: The Sulfur Caldron in the area of the Mud Volcano is a great example of a bubbling mudpot. NPS photo by Harlan Kredit.

Below: The Fishing Bridge has been closed to fishing since 1973 and it now a popular spot to look for cutthroat trout. NPS photo by J. Schmidt.

Geyser to cook it! In the spring and early summer, when the water level in the lake is higher, the Fishing Cone may actually be submerged underwater. But when the cone is above the surface of the lake, the water inside the geyser is boiling and you can often see steam rising from within the cone.

A nice hike in this area is the Duck Lake Trail, located near Grant Village. You can climb a small hill for views of Duck Lake and Yellowstone Lake. You can also see the effects of the massive fires of 1988 that swept through this part of the park.

Above: Fishing Cone in the West Thumb Geyser Basin. Early visitors to Yellowstone claimed to catch fish in the lake then quickly dip them in the boiling water of this geyser to cook them. NPS Photo by Jim Peaco.

> *Did you know that about three million people visit Yellowstone National Park each year?*

But Wait ... There's More: Things to Do and See Outside the Park

In addition to the fun and exciting attractions within Yellowstone National Park, there are many interesting things to see and do just outside the boundaries of the park. You don't need to drive far to find more fun. Grand Teton National Park and the towns of West Yellowstone, Montana and Jackson Hole, Wyoming are very close to Yellowstone National Park.

West Yellowstone, MT: The town of West Yellowstone, Montana is located just outside the west entrance to the park. It has an old, rustic feel but also has modern attractions like a museum, many restaurants, shops, tours, and events that can make your vacation extra special.

The Grizzly and Wolf Discovery Center is a wildlife park and educational facility. It is located only about a block from the west entrance to Yellowstone. Here you can see wolves and grizzly bears up close and learn about their habitats, diets and other general facts about the

Yellowstone ecosystem. You can learn more about the Discovery Center at www.grizzlydiscoveryctr.org.

Also located just outside the west entrance to Yellowstone is the Yellowstone IMAX Theatre. Here you can watch an IMAX film called "Yellowstone" and see interesting displays located in the lobby. During the film, Yellowstone's history, geothermal activity, and wildlife will come to life on a larger-than-life IMAX screen. It's fun for both children and adults. You can learn more about the IMAX Theatre at www.yellowstoneimax.com.

The Junior Smokejumper Program is a free, educational program that tells the story of smokejumpers and fire ecology. Smokejumpers are firefighters who specialize in parachuting to fires in remote area. The classes are modeled after the Junior NASA Programs and are designed for children between age five and twelve. They are held at the city park in West Yellowstone, Montana most days during July and August. Junior Smokejumper candidates are introduced to fire suppression methods and techniques that smokejumpers use to control and suppress forest and range fires. You can learn more about this program at www.smokejumpercenter.com.

Grand Teton National Park: Wyoming's Grand Teton Mountain, the centerpiece of Grand Teton National Park, is a sight that is hard to forget. Along with the other peaks in the mountain range, it rises over seven thousand feet above the flat valley below. Because there are no foothills in front of the mountains, the view is dramatic. But the mountains aren't the only natural attraction that makes

Grand Teton National Park so spectacular. It also has gleaming lakes, meadows filled with wildflowers, and lots of wildlife.

As you leave Yellowstone National Park through the southern entrance, you will follow the John D. Rockefeller Memorial Parkway right into Grand Teton National Park. John D. Rockefeller, Jr. was one of the richest men who ever lived. His father started one of the world's largest oil companies. John D. Rockefeller, Jr. used much of his family's money to purchase land that would benefit generations to come. In fact he bought land for some of America's greatest national parks including Grand Teton, Great Smoky Mountain National Park, and Acadia National Park.

There are many things to do in Grand Teton National Park. If you're interested in hiking, try the Heron Pond or Swan Lake trails along the banks of Jackson Lake. The trails start just south of Colter Bay (grab a map in the Visitor Center). These are both easy trails through wetland areas that will give you great views of the park. You may also see trumpeter swans or moose while on your hike.

If you prefer boating, during the summer months Jenny Lake Boating offers a boat shuttle service to the Cascade Canyon Trailhead across Jenny Lake or scenic cruises around the lake. If you take the shuttle to the Cascade Canyon Trailhead you can then hike a short trail past Hidden Falls to Inspiration Point. Jenny Lake Boating also rents kayaks and canoes at the Jenny Lake boat launch. You can learn more about boat rentals and shuttles at www.jennylakeboating.com.

Another option during the summer is to take an aerial tram in Teton Village. The ride up is fun and once you get off at the top, you can hike around the mountaintop before riding back down. You can learn more about the aerial tram at www.jacksonhole.com.

Jackson Hole, WY: The town of Jackson Hole, Wyoming lies just south of Grand Teton National Park. If you visit Grand Teton, it is worth a trip into town. There are shops and restaurants but one of the best things to see is the Jackson Hole town square. In the center of the town square is a park that takes up an entire block. In each corner of the park is a tall antler arch, made of real elk antlers gathered from the National Elk Refuge just north of town. It's a great spot for a family photo.

NPS photo

Conclusion, Checklists and Word Games

Congratulations! After reading this book, you probably know more than your parents about the geology, history, and natural attractions in Yellowstone National Park. You can use your knowledge to help your family plan a memorable trip to Yellowstone. Decide what you want to see and do then start packing! You can use the packing list in this section to help you prepare for your trip. This section also contains an animal checklist and some word games and puzzles to keep you busy and entertained. Have fun and remember that we all play a part in protecting and preserving Yellowstone and all of America's national parks. Follow the rules, stay on the trails, and don't litter or get too close to wildlife. Most of all, enjoy Yellowstone!

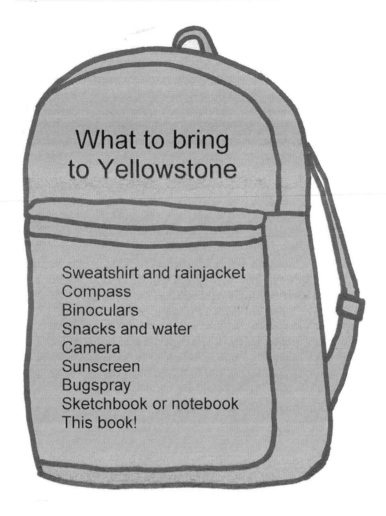

What to bring to Yellowstone

Sweatshirt and rainjacket
Compass
Binoculars
Snacks and water
Camera
Sunscreen
Bugspray
Sketchbook or notebook
This book!

NPS drawing by Robert Hynes

Following is a list of animals you may see in Yellowstone. You can check off the animals you see and write down the date and location where each one was spotted.

❑ Bald Eagle _____

❑ Beaver _____

❑ Bighorn Sheep _____

❑ Bison _____

❑ Black Bear _____

❑ Bobcat _____

❑ Coyote _____

❑ Elk _____

❑ Golden Eagle _____

❑ Grizzly Bear _____

❑ Lynx _____

❑ Moose _____

❑ Mountain Lion (Cougar) _____

❑ Mule Deer _____

❑ Osprey _____

❑ Pronghorn Antelope _____

❑ Trumpeter Swan _____

❑ Wolf _____

Yellowstone's Wildlife

```
N  R  O  T  B  E  P  E  E  E  M  O
A  N  E  E  B  E  N  C  N  S  E  E
W  O  T  I  E  I  A  N  E  R  O  H
S  R  E  T  O  O  S  R  P  G  M  M
R  M  R  E  M  R  W  O  L  F  C  S
E  O  R  O  S  T  B  H  N  B  C  S
T  O  R  B  O  M  Y  G  L  O  O  T
E  S  W  E  R  C  R  N  Y  G  G  T
P  E  E  H  S  N  R  O  H  G  I  B
M  R  L  Y  O  O  T  R  R  T  E  E
U  A  K  G  Y  E  R  P  S  O  S  A
R  L  F  N  A  H  P  E  S  O  S  Y
T  Y  R  O  W  E  O  E  E  I  E  R
V  U  L  M  O  M  Y  E  R  P  S  O
```

WOLF	OSPREY
ELK	BIGHORN SHEEP
COYOTE	PRONGHORN
EAGLE	TRUMPETER SWAN
BISON	MOOSE
BEAR	OSPREY

Natural Wonders of Yellowstone

```
B N B E E N O C K N I P O K F
V M A G N I R P S T O H E R U
S E S I O A E L T S A C F L M
R A T A C T G R S H E L D I A
I P M N G N T F N M U E N B R
V S R T N U Y E O F E E O E O
E L V E I O A D H N R N T R L
R L E S H F E T I V A O A T E
S A C S S T I T A C P R O Y R
I F C C I A R S L D E E B C R
D R F H F E P O U S O R M A P
E E W D V R V M Y S R O A P S
R W L A I G B E E H I V E F L
M O R N I N G G L O R Y T O N
I T G I B B O N F A L L S R V
E X C E L S I O R Y S I A D N
```

BEEHIVE	FISHING CONE	FUMAROLE
CASTLE	GIBBON FALLS	OLD FAITHFUL
DAISY	GREAT FOUNTAIN	TRAVERTINE
EXCELSIOR	HOT SPRING	PINK CONE
GIANTESS	LIBERTY CAP	RIVERSIDE
GEYSER	MINERVA SPRING	STEAMBOAT
MUDPOT	MORNING GLORY	TOWER FALLS
VOLCANO	WHITE DOME	

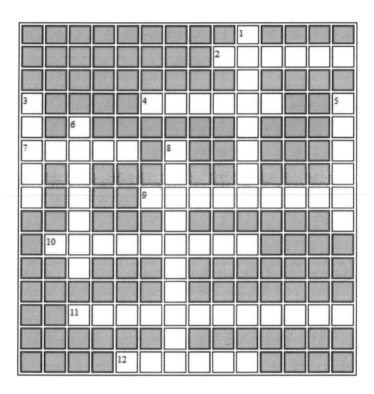

Across

2. Similar to a hot spring except the groundwater has dissolved the rocks into clay.
4. _____ Moran drew some of the first pictures of Yellowstone.
7. President of the United States who signed the act creating Yellowstone National Park.
9. Type of pine tree with cones that are glued shut with resin.
10. Fastest land animal in North America.
11. Microscopic living organisms that live in hot springs.
12. A member of the Lewis and Clark expedition who later explored Yellowstone.

Down

1. A steam vent in the earth's crust.
3. Hot molten rock.
5. Led an expedition to the Yellowstone area in 1871.
6. A depression or large, shallow hole in the earth's surface.
8. Means related to the heat within the earth.

About the Author

Stephanie Del Grande has traveled extensively throughout the United States, visiting many of the country's national parks over the past thirty years. As a child she toured the United States with her two brothers, parents, and grandmother in their family's pop-up camper. Fond childhood memories of these trips led to a deep interest in America's national parks. As an adult, Stephanie now explores the country with her husband and two school age children.

Resources

Fuller, Steven and Schmidt, Jeremy. 1990. *Yellowstone Grand Teton Road Guide.* Jackson Hole, WY: Free Wheeling Guides.

Repanshek, Kurt. 2006. *Frommer's National Parks with Kids.* Hoboken, NJ: Wiley Publishing, Inc.

National Park Service Official Web Site for Yellowstone National Park. http://www.nps.gov/yell

Yellowstone Association Official Web Site. http://www.yellowstoneassociation.org

Yellowstone Digital Slide File Home Page. http://www.nps.gov/archive/yell/slidefile/index.htm

Index

978-0-595-47973-3
0-595-47973-1